SKELETON OF LIGHT

SKELETON OF LIGHT

BY
THOMAS VANCE

Chapel Hill
THE UNIVERSITY OF NORTH CAROLINA PRESS

CONTEMPORARY POETRY SERIES

Copyright © 1946, 1947, 1948, 1950, 1952, 1954, 1956, 1957, 1959, 1960, 1961
by Thomas Vance

The poems "New England Nocturne," "The Masque of the Chase," and, in somewhat different form, "The Round of Spring," appeared originally in *The New Yorker*. Some of the other poems appeared previously in *The Atlantic Monthly, The Dartmouth Literary Quarterly, Discovery, Hip-Pocket Poems, The Nation, The New York Times, Poetry,* and *The Yale Review*.

Dedication: *TO VERA*

Inward your eyes
Made the terror open
Undid the mere midnight
Taught time to the bone

Through the strange fire
Your lips listening
Interpreted the tongues
Cracked the crypt of war
And let the root sing
The rock answer the sun

PREFACE

Pointless as Plato
To speak of poetry: no one
In reason affords
A mere first habit

A mere potion
(A form of poison)
Trickling all this time
Clearly with no improvement

From the first, primitive
Imaginary
But much talked of transparence
Of those four famous rivers

Or better the first
Sap rising and rounding
Ripening and reddening
The flowering fruit

Before the serpent forked
His tongue or Eve found
Terror or Adam
Dreamed Eve to be

Anything but deathless
A doll by the clock
Of heaven's finger
Every day exactly

At dawn waking
At noon smiling
At midnight making
Believe, and knew her

Alive with a difference
Dying for good.

CONTENTS

Dedication: To Vera
Preface

DOUBLE EDGE
Song of the Dark Wood	3
Love's Leisure	5
The Wall	6
Perils of Convalescence	8
What Sun Is Burning	9
Love's End	11

NOONS AND SEASONS
Still to Begin	13
The Round of Spring	14
The May Day of the Wisewoman	16
Solstice	17
The Noon of Loss	18
New England Nocturne	19
Woman in an Empty House	20
The Stroke of Noon	21

GUESTS, STATUES, KINGS
A Statue Is a Solid Ghost	23
On the Difficulty of Justice	25
Pastoral Ballet	26
Guests at Midnight	28
The Plumbing of the Kings	30
Disillusion of Six O'Clock	32
Autobiography of a Statue	33

LEGEND
The Masque of the Chase	37
The Maiden Shrouded as a Deer	38
Kerstin and the Bridegroom	40
Legend	42
The Stream	43
The Lady and the Ghost	45
Figures in a Garden	46

STRIKING A BALANCE
Moment of Peril	47
Instant in the Eye	48
Poise of Light	50
Morning Song	51
Striking a Balance	52
The Catch	54
At the Shadow's Heart	56

SKELETON OF LIGHT

DOUBLE EDGE

SONG OF THE DARK WOOD

While purest danger poured
From the dead nightingale,
Every hushed leaf
Uttered its hurting spell

Far in the high forest,
I woke no track or sign,
But heard to unlock the dark
The bending wisewoman,

The blind one, who with weeds
Had greened her body of oak:
To hear her humming tongue
I hung bloodless as rock,

And caught on the stopped wind
With what simplicity
She cleft my vacant heart
And filled my lidded eye:

"Through the singing wood
In the shadow of a grief
Pierced by delight remembered,
You move, reaching for life

Where blossoms globe the air,
Yet take from wizened trees
The round fruit of anguish,
The apple ripe with reason,

Whose taste is mortal yet
Mysterious beyond nature
Wakes mere bone, marrow's wit,
Breathes, bloods you, burning creature:

How lost past loss you'll live
Closed in careful walls
A season of still leaves
Where no sleep, no light falls,

A night of black flowers
Whence time itself has flown—
The dial tells there no hours,
The glass no stars, no bird

Yet stirs the naked dawn:
There, past the enchanted night,
Stares, hushed beyond approach,
The skeleton of light."

LOVE'S LEISURE

It was to learn the simplest word
Never
The sunlight of the beginning
Time beyond touch
Now, close as the heart's pulse
The breath, focus of being
First home's hearth, the pit
Marked by the X
The leaping cross, the rock
Opening, world without end
The world's end.

THE WALL

This wall that steals like an exhalation

Keeps closing around me in the summer air
Through which I trace the fronds of ferns without stems
And am conscious of lives, of men, of friends, those saving faces
Floating like masks

Shadows me noiselessly through rooms, and on roads
Slides hung in the atmosphere to deceive my sense
Denying the hill, the looks of towns and turns of valleys
The sudden flower by the field

This wall, conjured from cloud, mere magic

Mortared of subtlest stones of mist,
Heavier than marble and tall as that cliff, the end
That, blind as a conqueror, reason could waste and calmly pass
And come back saying nothing

For moments can melt and cave beneath a faint
Astonishing shaft of sunlight, reminding me of beginnings
Then only of clocks, to perform by day and still at evening
To enter the mirror and fix my nails

This wall, established in dreams

At midnight moves and grows, shrinking my bed
Towering in transparent blackness through which hope's eye
Cold, pure and strange as the star of a new pole
Pierces the dark absence of sleep

This mystery of substance, hell's shadow
Sprang from the earth shaken by love, to lift
For a countless time my centered prison, my cell rooted
To drink the rain of quickening loss

This wall, wild sleight, air's wisdom

Is skilled to school me yet in the end
Of anguish, to suffer rejoicing, in houses not my own
In trees, stones, wars, the light and terrible grounds of being
Love's center killed, forever springing

This wall that cancels the open world of touch, of suns
Contracts me now to a more intrinsic burning
This wall that breathes from hell, that kills my love
Cleaves me past death, that only my love may live.

PERILS OF CONVALESCENCE

Sometimes the circling knives that ghost my head
Each edged with the glittering curve of error
Each whetted to kill a man
Cease like a nightmare's murder of nothing
And I have the quiet of cattle or stillest grass
With no conscience drinking the sky and the world's streams.

Sometimes the singing wound that quickening weakens
That which yet lives of my heart
Is sealed up in silence and sudden wholeness
Steals over me like a tree's fibre and leaves
All terror hidden: I am no more divided but one
Speechless in death like any plant or stone.

WHAT SUN IS BURNING

This suffering grows like a tree.
On its towering leaves light could kindle forever,
But I cannot lift up my eyes to regard them.
Its roots, which I see, are dark and dive downward
To drink subterranean rivers that yesterday,
When with drills I entered that vault of shadows,
Were not there,
To cleave and take life from the heart of rocks
That yesterday, when I attempted them with hammers,
Would not yield.

This suffering, being a tree in the world's acres,
Yet sends out spiritual roots into the air.
One takes the heart from my body
And buries it in unknown ground
To become the food of that which transforms it.
I had died but now,
But now breathe and rejoice,
Being opened and fastened by invisible threads
To all that lies hidden, that, though dark as evil, lost,
Yet lives, and endures to mirror the light.

Still sometimes when the wind spoke
The man I was, the man I shall be in time again
(Tomorrow, another dying yesterday),
Trembled at this tree's gentlest trembling.
What spectral radiance hovered over its head
Known on the frozen ground by reflection only,
Each of its thousand ghosts of branches
Whispering a keener shade of life's terror?

I woke and cried, surprising nothing.

Forever my voice vanishes,
And quiet beyond my slipping fear,
Beyond my uncertain edges, cliffs of sleep,
Under the sky that showers an altered light,
This suffering's mystery grows, its roots of air
And earth, cool fingers, light as flowers
To bind the breasts of men with living wounds,
Cleaving the bones of eternal yesterday.

How close to death
This suffering, this visible and invisible tree,
Opens the earth before my unstirring eyes.
Its roots bind my receiving body to the rocks.
Its shade withers and quickens the daily grass.
Its leaves, which cover the sky, forbid me yet
To behold what sun is burning.

LOVE'S END

I

It was a casual stroke
Ending the summer hour.
I turned, and the leaves turned,
Your beauty froze in the air.

I thought slowly to freeze
To the root lost, and live
Weeping one storm to drown
The heaven's lightning of love.

Locked time! When clocks of tears
Had sluiced my power to feel,
Dry horror, night's hooded judge,
Condemned me to his wheel.

Pinioned, the polestar split,
My riddling conscience whirled;
Wounds, wells, quick chasms, cried
To drink me and the world.

Yet on my end of earth
Your act of Eden fell;
Again your part of grace
Was whole, and lighted hell.

II

Then surely I died, except
A saving sheet of ice
Spread darkly over my sense
Its white eternities.

Numb, cold, how rapt from death
I slept on nothing's bed;
Once in that absence quick,
I dreamed your vanishing head,

And other visions, ghosts,
The caved shadow of Christ,
On waters without weight
Walked, and I rose, a ghost.

Trembling brought back my flesh,
Yet lights frosted like stars
From distance like my room
Pierced burning through my fears.

Did I live? Lost as one
Who has been blind, and sees,
I bore how winter's poles
Compass the burning rose.

III

I woke my frozen feet
And learned to walk again,
Though daily I fell, struck
Nerveless as air or stone.

And broke thirst's barrier.
That desert's bright zero
Taught shriveled heart, chilled flower,
To unlock a well of fire.

Beneath the pouring sun
I limped in the earth's dance,
Stripped, suffering, all in time,
The blade of radiance.

If I had blood, it sang
Mere terror's end, to prove
Against death's simple edge
The double edge of love

That still beyond all wounds
Pierces the body of man
With light to make flesh whole
And knit the fractured bone.

NOONS AND SEASONS

STILL TO BEGIN

The poet for whom the golden age
Fell every hour,
Being buried with a dead idiom, tripped
The lost scholar.

But to stay essential man against
The impostor, time,
The emperor bound all men, yoked beasts,
To exalt his tomb.

Still bridegroom and bride at midnight took
The shining bed,
But woke when morning froze and touched
Their bodies dead.

Even, I have heard, in ageless heaven
Bright yesterday,
Freezing perfection, burns to catch
The backward eye.

Even, they say, the angels' song
Wins by loss,
Hymning what radiance before hell
Taught paradise.

Difficult yet on earth fallen
Still to begin
The end that sang with earliest stars
The birth of man.

THE ROUND OF SPRING
(April, 1944)

Light tilts the pole, and strikes
With sudden daffodil
Thin cities, roses in glass
The snake on the brightening hills.

New birds clamor the air,
New boys on echoing lawns
Cry havoc, singing war,
And grow tall in the sun.

Now seven seas stream bright,
The shark is smoother-skinned,
The minnow in clearer cove
Hangs gold above the sand,

While inland the long south wind
Through distant valley rides,
Cuts off the ice, and flanks
The arctic mountainside.

Now free, the highest field
Draws green from sun and seed;
Against the greener branch
The tanager starts like blood.

Projects that slept like trees
Put forth their shoots again;
The bending general
Pricks home his far campaign,

Whose pawns, pinned heroes, wheel
Wide as the course of whales,
Or past the horizon's curve
In conquering tempest fall.

Now poet or lover wins
New visions of the sun,
From roses, themselves: new sense;
And now the prudent man

Keeps quiet in his heart
A green thicket of briars,
Three adders in his breast,
An owl behind his eyes,

To outstare that frosty ghost
Who looks through the rose,
Who smiles to see the smile
That lights the murdering seas;

Whose silence sings beyond
The sudden daffodil,
The scarlet leaf, the thin shade,
The whitening of the hills.

THE MAY DAY OF THE WISEWOMAN

Today when the cock crew and blew out the clock
I decided not to keep house with caution:
I intend to waltz and sing a cracked song,
And the King, trumpeting Death himself, shall not prevent me.

For today, traveling with all his sleights of light,
He strides like a wizard out of the bright horizon;
He has woven flowers into his hair and shimmering beard,
And thrushes are singing on his shoulders.

His cheek is made up like any cherub's, red and white;
He is dripping with dew and the dust of gardens.
Ha! My old cane has sprouted a green leaf,
And so I tumble to meet my ancient friend.

SOLSTICE

Still summer climbs the dark of brooks
Lighting the ghostly wildflower in
The cool crevice; still cool, the moss
Stanches with green the seeping stone,

And still, slowly, the rivers sink,
The roots are searching; stretched in the sun,
The airy veins of leaves grow stiff,
The dayspring green with birds is flown.

Rich weddings give themselves and go.
The complete rose wilts in the glass.
Bridegroom and bride are locked to storm
The quiet of their longer kiss.

Hills, orchards curve from flower to fruit.
The high noon hesitates, then falls
Slowly. Quiet on dusty light
The keen transparent shadow steals.

THE NOON OF LOSS

Tall silence vaults the air;
Summer, still, shafts the yard;
Storms are beyond, and fear
A whisper guessed, not heard.

The widow stands at noon
Alone in the shining garden.
The sheer sun by the hollyhock
Suspends the hummingbird.

Now she will never stir
But strange by staring grow
Mortised in ground of stone,
Tenoned, a stiller tree,

Transfixing time with time
As first and last were now,
As instant sight should pierce
No more to become, but be.

So caught, she has slipped sense
Of sunlit border-stone,
Touched by a point of shade;
But now, the bright bird flown,

Breath stirs, an oak's first leaf
For autumn winds to earth,
An insect starts in the air,
And death again has birth.

NEW ENGLAND NOCTURNE

The valley's curve
Sinks shaded, yet
Cool spire, stone mill
Burn in sunset.

From leaning trees
Two last leaves twirl
Slow, balanced, caught;
Slow waters swirl

Already half seen;
The shadowy tide
Of different night
Begins to glide,

To steal thresholds;
Soon it will drown
The fires on windows,
Soon will bring down

The burning branch
Of sumac, still
Crimson on rock;
Soon it will kill

The last reflection
Of summer, caught
Glassed on stone rivers;
Soon, in still night,

While old rooftrees
Sink back in woods
Where farms are shut
By vanishing roads,

Pines, hills will drift
Dark, acres lost,
And skies of stars
Burn white with frost.

WOMAN IN AN EMPTY HOUSE

Bright meadows fall in shade
To chilling stones of streams;
Still afternoon is stretched
With echoes, thin perfumes.

Long, slow, through hollow walls,
Through ceilings bare as sky,
She has singled the bright leaf
That burned on the dark bough.

But evening's quietest edge
Shivers the autumn air;
All seasons slip; love's wit
Asks secrets, things that are.

Noon, ages, brought her news.
Since, nothing's image has
Grown on her inward eye
Like silence on the grass.

Silence has sealed the sun;
Trees, rocks are rooted still;
The hills look steady, stars
Wheel slow around the pole,

As if the world, being sure,
Need not set terror loose,
But held in perfect form
The poise of emptiness

Shattered. Fallen, ashen leaves
Are cradling the cold seed;
The Bear, stripped, still as ice,
Yet burns the summer's blood.

Fearful, essential selves,
All fires spring quick again,
Whose radiance, nothing's death,
Shivers the spectral stone.

THE STROKE OF NOON

al medio día, que es la eternidad

Still shafts, substantial light,
Tented the field,
As stream's bend, stone, noon's tree
Paused: the blind pulse was stilled.

Depth glowing hallowed the ground;
The hollow of peace
Burned upward through quick rock
And clouds that combed the grass.

None needed the clock's finger
To search his wound,
Nor bird's nor shade's flight
To whisper of man's end.

None needed war's blade
To exact his blood:
That air past violence
Anchored its sharper seed.

The meadow's quiet could storm
The iciest seas,
Waking the monstrous world
To unseal the towers of cries.

It was for life, for death,
Yet was not long,
As if man's choice were light
And the bare cliff could sing.

GUESTS, STATUES, KINGS

A STATUE IS A SOLID GHOST

> *La peinture est notre art, et la sculpture celui que nous avons ressuscité; c'est pourquoi celle-ci semble parfois l'âme impérieuse de la plus lointaine histoire, le symbole du vieil Homme interrogateur des astres....*
>
> André Malraux

They blow away like newspapers
The officers of the day, the orators
In frock coats crusted with smog

All the decaying angels. Beyond
Their gestures under the puffing pigeons
There is a quieter speech of stone.

A statue is a solid ghost
Breath vanishing into marble
Whose lightest grace has gravity

It is god, hero or, stranger, man
With eyes open in rigor mortis
Looking out of a further light

Questioning the eyelid's flutter
That lives, and keeps its pulse in time
To shut itself against the dark

A statue in the morning market is bankrupt
Toppled easily by a child's breath
Yet finds its living in man's dying

And rises like the oldest conqueror
Curved under his heavy arms
Stunned by the stars, climbing slowly

Out of the cellar of the seventh buried city
To haunt the stairs of a new house
With images abolished at daybreak

Or sometimes watches from a high roof
Roman or timeless with his empire
Worrying the world asleep in its low ceilings

Sometimes a lover, motionless
Moving beyond the killing mirror
Fixed where he stood with instant beauty

Sometimes the man of no man's peace
The word lifted with each new weapon
Nailed to the giving of his grace

A statue is a stricken ghost
Yet, brotherly, shares his wound
The stroke sent shivering through the mind

Heaven's sightless edge in time that breaks
The body of blood and makes it new
Quiet and immortal as a stone.

ON THE DIFFICULTY OF JUSTICE
A song for Jonathan Swift

All the wars were filed away;
The cool of reason fixed the sky.

All the stars were measured, yet
The unmeasured pole itself had set.

Dark and echoing hung the peace
That held me like an empty house,

When I heard single in the air
My buried brother singing there,

And listening, caught, caught by surprise
The strain of ancient harmonies:

"My heaven is shot, my world is split,
The worm is dancing in my wit;

"My hair, my flesh, my skin are gone;
I am a naked skeleton,

"Yet I can dress up for a feast,
Masking in glass, the mirror's ghost.

"I have seen my shadow slain
Buried to rise to breathe again;

"The burning winds have spun my dust,
But I have kept the lust I lost;

"The burning feet have sprung my eyes,
While yet I watched, a cold witness.

"Of every quick promise that ends
I sing with lightest spirits for friends;

"My mother, lover, son being dead,
I sleep with spectres in my bed;

"Still I can stare polite and mild
Questioning like any child,

"And I can kill to keep my pride,
As if I had never died."

PASTORAL BALLET

> *Howl, ye shepherds, and cry.*
> Jeremiah

> *The play thou schouburgst, Game, here endeth.*
> Finnegans Wake

The trees stood high and held their figs.
Still as white boulders on the grass
The sheep were planted; every day
The purest sun would come to pass.

Then rainbows wheeled on every cloud.
Through hollow space since the deluge
The shepherds piped their witching tunes.
The prophet, terrible on time's edge,

Sang how the hosts would flame and fall,
The holiest cities sleep, buried.
The silly sheep were munching still.
The prophet tapped his skull and cried.

It was swift that the sculptured kings
Moved freezing by in high relief:
Beneath their brazen feet the green
Pastures ran blood for very life.

Heavenly the pose the shepherds held!
The prophet was stiff to understand
The light that pierces the lost world.
His book was burning in his hand.

How slow the ancient hills dissolved!
The rivers slipped, the grass was gone;
The immortal shepherds minced their ease
In paper or pretty porcelain.

High, dying lion, the prophet paced,
Publishing to the wind. The stones
And sand recovered him like a sea.
His quick ghost thundered from his bones.

The shepherds, princely figurines,
Danced light in heaven on doomsday.
The towering prophet, whirling cloud,
Shattered the finish of their play.

The masque is stripped; the prophet's stroke
Cleaves open new heaven and new earth:
Loud as a flood the whirling flocks
Of men come crying back to birth.

GUESTS AT MIDNIGHT

When I was younger I dreamed in my house of glass,
"All's fair in love and hate, war and the world,
As long as there's tomorrow left for thinking."
I thought, while tomorrows traveled through the mirror,
"The private dream, cocoon-protection, split,
Man, ego and mortality, crawls out,
Insect with summer wings, to die in secret,
Still to be born, to take a stiffer spring."
Now in my stiffening danger I remember
The birth of four young men, deserted the womb,
The incubating walls and moonlit gardens,
To weigh the ringing world, the alien fact,
Against a singled conscience.

                                                First from the first
Bowed gently and found contentment smiling
At dinner, turning with the clock discreetly,
Dying without suspicion.

                                The next, more nearly conscious,
Withdrew, praying, and was lost, mentioned
Only in retrospect, parenthesis
In the preoccupation of uneasy friends.

The third, knowing as if completely, except
The hollow of his marrow, made to meet
An age of iron with his mother's milk.
Time curdled him in his glass; seeing himself
A conscious fool among unconscious knaves,
He tossed on his bed all night, resolving violence.
A new man at breakfast, at noon sunlit,
He took a smart increase in income, with smiles
Redoubled later, while he died with millions;
A frequent funeral, not remembered.

                                                     The last
Was sure, declined to compromise, spoke out,
Heard the applause, his own voice echoing, rose,
A shirt-front gleaming from the height of banquets,
And was buried with honor.

                        In the caverns of my brain
Their ghosts meet at midnight, thin with knowledge,
Famished for the spent sun.

                    But the sun burns.

THE PLUMBING OF THE KINGS

Gloucester: *O let me kiss that hand!*

Lear: *Let me wipe it first; it smells of mortality.*

I

Le Roi Soleil, fresh, laced with perfumes,
Yet uttered odors from his skin
That filled, they say, the palace rooms,
And made his flatterers wince within.

The Faery Queen was maid of flesh:
Cold, courtiers of Elizabeth
In secret saw her fading face
Beneath the incense watch for death.

All forms, I've read, all favors fail,
The apparent heir wears out his suit;
Now father's will nor thread of womb
Can stitch the ruined absolute.

Then quick, Promethean reason soars,
Calls out the naked Puritan
To print on worlds, white, blank as charts,
Sudden in blood, the Rights of Man.

II

How is the Seeker lost who finds!
His way beneath the burning eye
Of heaven makes money, all his shares
Of history hedged, his future high.

He shifts, the scalping pioneer,
The brave, the baron of the mine,
Perfumes his reeking hands, and prays
His shining great-grandson to dine.

Behold a modern wonder! King
Is the washed child with wife for queen:
These with a nicer pride receive
The flattery of the machine.

The daily bath renews the skin
The elevators wing the feet
The ice-cubes in the enameled box
Can keep beer cool and butter sweet.

III

In front of Shakespeare's father's house
In Stratford stood a pile of dung
Whose smells rose mingling with the spring
When Shakespeare's brain was quick and young,

Who yet remembered, studying deep
The ironic question, poised with fear,
To meditate the mortal sweat
That seized the anointed flesh of Lear.

The stable fails: the mineral scent
Of gasoline is on the streets;
Alone in glass and steel the man
Remains the animal who eats,

And pours his refuse, sterilized,
Beneath the city to the sea
To keep the averted nostrils sealed
From odors of mortality.

IV

Golden, the plumber shores the pipes
That twist beneath the glistening tiles,
And where the skyway gleams, the girl
Glides over the fuming rubbish piles.

The King floats on his rubber chair,
Bent to the whisper of the screen
That tells him softly what to wear,
The caves of earth, the submarine.

Say Shakespeare's eye returns to tent
The infected soul beneath the face,
And pierce the metal vanities
That skin and film the ulcerous place,

But the more prudent man of means
Keeps surfaces that keep from death
And floats imperial to the end
Of Louis and Elizabeth.

DISILLUSION OF SIX O'CLOCK

Leaflight, outleaping Ram and Bull
Enters the room to cleave the smoke
Catches the smile, the dead cocktail
And gives the eye a greener look.

That couple lacquered in their corner
Aging and young in careful clothes
Though barely speaking to each other
Yet keep intense their speaking pose

Have made each other and have nothing
Left to make except love or
Nothing to do for a new spring
But not to make love any more.

AUTOBIOGRAPHY OF A STATUE

I

Weeds garland my hair: cold light, warm rain
Have caved my eyes and chipped the chiseled style
That once proclaimed my stony death forever.

Midsummer lightning has snapped my lifted hand.
Now my good arm drips slowly to the soil.
The sap of grass climbs to my knees, my tongue.

It is as if the oldest stone of knowledge
Floated, new-formed, within the watery womb.
Once I too leapt howling into the light.

II

Crying to touch, my hands shaping the air,
I learned to smile beneath my golden halo
And crawled from the crib into the speaking house.

There was my mother, dreaming while I watched.
With "da da da" I stuttered into the alphabet
From "am" and "baby" to the book of zebras.

Now I could bomb the air with eloquence
Until the table quailed, the walls receded,
The rug was my rock on which I stood in wrath.

A three-foot king, I stripped the devil of space,
And seeing the nothing of my adversary
Swept with my flags across the nursery floor.

Still in the yard the Christmas snowman stood;
April brought back the names of singing birds
And the autumn bonfire laughed on the same lawn.

How soon my eyes walked higher than the hedge!
My troops fought, broken, for my foolish brother;
The fall of flowers in time brought a new whisper.

If first my face burned like an injured cherub's
Washed by the bully in the gritty snow,
I turned, grown tall, myself the bully hero.

Captive, I halted through the playing schools,
Rhyming the curls of girls, spelling the words
That hunt the cunning dead out of their caves.

I combed my hair and hid my usual secrets,
Until the quick glass caught me by the beard:
My mother smiled her pride, in time weeping.

In time my father spoke: "It is time to think
The cost of living, the parades of war,
The point of angels, yes, the end of man.

"Is it for nothing that the marble fathers
Walled in the islands, froze the slipping poles?
Here is your history, how quick blood is tombed.

"Here are the books that build the burning stone.
Here is the storm, and here the star that steals."
In death his face froze, far as any statue's.

Had I not studied the nice rules of grammar?
My words were brave in show, but still my bone
Declined the missing part of speech, death's silence.

III

My baggage packed, I left the house grown hollow,
Hungry for air: I could eat anything,
Newspapers, cobwebs, pocked films of the moon.

In the cramped park, between the crumbling statues,
She stood, that near one, vanishing, radiant as
The illumination in a book's margin.

It was then that the sightless structure of light
Hung shining and as if solid in the curves of air.
The oak's shadow was pierced, the buildings changed.

A year, an hour, we walked as light as dancers;
I was magnificent with my absent money;
Leashed to her wrist she led the beasts of legend.

In the dull park, dusted with summer sunset,
My love glowed like a manikin, her face of wax.
I cried (because it never had been she),

"O love on whose lightest head the heavens had rested
Where are your living eyes, reverted now,
Sealed to the sightless vision of a mask?"

She listened, quiet, electric as a kitten.
Neither the streetlight nor the polestar trembled.
I looked and saw my feet had lost their shoes,

And, wrapt in windy danger, bare, in rags,
I walked the open world on tilting planks,
On smoothest streets stumbling into forests.

An hour, a year, I looked back, quick as nightmare,
And shaped myself, a pillar of weeping glass,
Crystal to hold the instant of my ending,

Until the world in labor, big with lightning,
Broke on my head with its enormous storm
And washed my eyes into its saltier sea.

My warlike prowess, how I broke the codes,
Seeing the armies burned in the draft of absence,
And in my skeleton caught the mortal cough,

How I came back, was feasted by new friends,
Became the consul and the burgomaster,
Added new fire-words to the frozen index,

How well I wore my elected face, that slowly
My features found themselves noble in stone,
My body's mineral flowering like a Roman,

Is nothing new; nor was the glory I witnessed:
While one invented a new vegetable
One found a weapon to explode the sun.

And now, my head salted with frost, the birds
Drink up the wit, airy as any nothing
That streams forever from my freezing beard.

But falling in fountains through their glittering song
Still I water like rain the roots of cities,
The wars of men seeking the quiet of stone.

LEGEND

THE MASQUE OF THE CHASE

(After Ulrich von Württemberg)

With cold despair my horn is wound;
The joy I had is vanished;
The wild shade flies light from the hound:
My hunt is forever finished.
And I had chosen from this forest
That I should honor alone
The loveliest and the noblest beast.
Now the sweet game is flown.

Fare forward, wild one, in the wood's delight!
With terror I'll never take you,
Nor graze your breast of snowiest white.
Another now must wake you
With hunting cries and teeth of dogs—
Then you'll be tamed for good.
Move secret here, my secret deer.
With sorrow I leave this wood.

THE MAIDEN SHROUDED AS A DEER

(After an early Swedish ballad)

A deer ran through the dark forest,
A glitter of gold on her breast.

"You may shoot the hart, the roe,
But let the golden hind go,"

The mother said, "Or shoot the sun,
But let the hind that's golden run."

The boy shouldered his cunning bow
And walked in the wood's shadow.

When he came where the leaves were dim
The hind played lightly before him.

He dropped his bow across his knee:
The hind was hidden by a tree.

He braced his bow against his foot:
The hind vanished beside a root.

He held the bow before his thigh:
The hind was moving in his eye.

Into the shade the arrow fled
And shot his own sister dead.

The boy threw off his gloves, and kneeled
To flay the carcass he had killed.

He cut the quarry at the throat
And touched his sister's golden coat.

He flayed the gold hind, head and neck,
And found his sister's golden lock.

He flayed the flank, and still shining
There was his sister's golden ring.

He cast his knife down on the earth,
And said, "The old woman's word was truth."

Against himself he bent his bow;
His heart received the straight arrow.

The cranes fly high over the wood,
Winging the south, gone home for good,

But who can fly from sorrow is blest;
And yet she wears a golden breast.

KERSTIN AND THE BRIDEGROOM

(After an early Swedish ballad)

Kerstin sheds tears and blood without a sound,
Weeping her bridegroom out of the dark ground;
She sleeps, she wakes and cries for him in secret.

At the door the lightest fingers knock:
"Wake up, little Kerstin, and undo the lock."

"But I am not expecting anyone;
At such an hour I can let no one in."

"Wake up, little Kerstin, and unlock the door:
I am your lover whom you loved before."

Her feet run lightly over the cold floor,
And swiftly her fingers lift the latch of the door.

She leads her guest by the hand to the red chair;
He is dark as darkest earth who once was fair.

She washes his feet in the clearest wine,
And after wipes them dry in white ermine.

Now in the deepest bed these two lie down,
Whispering together: they'll never sleep till dawn.

"Listen, little Kerstin, never weep for me:
I'll never come here again for you to see.

"But now I hear the cocks who stretch and crow;
Now it is time for a dead man to go."

Kerstin has risen up and put on her shoes,
And followed her lover through the long woods.

They cross the stream and come where graves are laid,
Suddenly his yellow hair begins to fade.

She sees the moon rising in the daylight,
And the dead man vanishing from her sight.

Kerstin sits down forever on the tomb:
"And here I shall sit until the trumpet of doom."

But under the ground she hears the dead man,
"Listen, little Kerstin, go home again,

"For every time you weep or wake from unrest,
The stream of bitter blood runs in my breast;

"But when your heart is glad and no longer grieves,
Then in my breast I feel the light rose-leaves."
She sleeps, she wakes and cries for him in secret.

LEGEND

(After the German of Klopstock)

I found her in the spring's shadow
And bound her light with leaves and flowers.
She felt nothing and was still sleeping.

I gazed at her: my life hung
In that gazing on her life.
I felt it well and knew nothing.

I whispered to her without speech,
My arm held a branch that whispered.
She woke from sleep to greater quiet.

She gazed at me: her life hung
In that gazing on my life.
Then the world moved light around us.

THE STREAM

It was a man of bone
Mirrored in air like glass
Hero, puppet or ghost
Sat piping on the grass

"Beneath the mountain's cliff
Where shadow and sunlight meet
My love grew like a tree
A stream sang at her feet

Whoever drank that stream
Would grow like the air, the stone
Time could not touch his eye
Nor find him, fiber or bone

I drank that water and changed
Crying to north and south
I would take my death again
For one kiss from her mouth

My love's smile in the air
Changed back my stone to blood
She stepped strange from the tree
The stream of mirrors flowed

I kissed her, eye and lip
And took my love to bed
All night the stream of light
Went singing overhead

All night the stream's light fell
Wearing the proud mountain
All night the midnight burned
The hour, the year, were gone

The year, the years sang by
The dancing tree was bare
The mountain shadow only
The rock the only flower

How quick my love had caught
My dream of deathless stone
The changes of her smile
Taught me to die again

Endless the caves of ice
Marbled the end of grief
Gathering sunlight: my love
Ghosted new flower, new leaf

Beneath the mountain's cliff
Where snow and summer meet
My love sings like a tree
The cold stream at her feet"

THE LADY AND THE GHOST

I can trick my cheek
And twist my hair:
Slow, the light climbs
A cold tomorrow.
The ice feeds the spring,
And flaming summer
Singes the leaves.
The end is never.

I stand alone
In my night-dress,
And see you there:
I slip my loss,
My face blossoms
A rose in dry briars;
Then the clock strikes
Its quiet terrors.

Or again, at noon,
Where the brook turns
Its shivering light
Through shades of ferns,
I thought I had guessed
Your tall shadow,
And then I turned,
Touched by a tree.

What is my fault?
As if for a crime
I have condemned myself
Quick from my tomb.
Is it that, being stone,
I can almost move,
And still, being lost,
Am bound to love?

FIGURES IN A GARDEN

They are not quite of stone,
Motionless, held in light,
This woman and this man.

And not of air they live
Quick, lovely in the noon
Filtering through green leaves,

Nor is he quite evil,
That serpent growing there,
Coiling his angel's will

To strike the stone, the air,
To sting the man to man
And salt the woman's tear,

But keeps a hovering look,
Knowing how, when he pours
His heavenly gift, to speak,

They'll taste, and, ignorant still,
Questioning what they are,
Will turn to flesh and fall.

STRIKING A BALANCE

MOMENT OF PERIL

Ancient and new as any sun
The absolute vision blinds the man

The towering tragedy that he praised apart
Has stooped to arrest his single heart

Caught dead in living light, in waking flesh
Condemned to a dream's annihilation

House, feature, future stripped to know
To take eternity on the nerve of now

Now he is nothing, yet is blood
Beating and heart quickening

And having no being yet has brain
Aching and bone asking

No strength but sinew stretched and clinging
To the world's end, the still beginning

INSTANT IN THE EYE

Some truths, like murder, stand
An instant in the eye;
Then darkness like the blood's
Slips over them, and they flee.

> Yet that clear burning proof
> How man, quick lover, kills,
> Lives yet, can light the bone,
> Or ever the horror falls.

Yes, yesterday I caught sense
Past self, blood's history,
Heard music to unscrew
Each dungeon with its cry:

> Could sing how crippled war
> Stumbling, yet wins to dance;
> Then, self a cripple, you
> Fell dumb with violence.

What is that towering look
Whose truth falls, lying light,
Arresting with still grace
Wolf, will, the world of night?

> I think, what makes man man,
> What breaks mortality,
> What, brief as Christ, condemns
> The impossible to be.

Then the fine thread of blood
Stitching the lidded eye,
Contracting vision's reach
To the white bone's frailty?

> Yet teaches fearful love
> And traps truth with a kiss
> And nails the all-speaking word
> Where speechless terrors cross.

How blood that films the sight
And yokes man to the beast
Is yet the spirit's delight
And clearest wine of Christ—

        To know this, man should shrink
        To an angelic eye,
        But, bodied, needs new sense,
        That blood itself should see.

Once in still deepening trees
I stood held at sunset
And watched with centered heart
The red and level light

Move through the shadowy leaves,
As vision pierced my blood
With incandescence, then
Failed with the darkening wood.

        Phoenix of loss, first light
        Flew from us, fabled bird,
        Whose song, still cleaving night,
        Failed, and was never heard;

        Yet fell, not failed, for yet
        That light's point, rooted seed,
        Stems with its flower of grace
        The darkest flow of blood.

POISE OF LIGHT

Where you are clothed in nakedness like the sun's
Not to be bare, a stone caught in a cold gallery,
Nor merely to burn like a bare self,
Breathing desire, hushed in the walls of danger,

Though you keep grace with marble or coolest bronze,
And, moving still, touch quick their ancient meanings,
That can outfreeze the iciest death,
And teach the vanishing sinew to spring on nothing,

And though you are from within, quiet
And luminous as a candle's slender body,
Whose heart is light before its substance burns,
Balancing the enormous dark on a flame's point,

Your beauty is beyond blood, yet keeps the blood:
Perfection's yesterday cannot freeze your motion,
Nor tomorrow's ignorance wound you, naked, still
Poised like the sun to hold the heaven's distance.

MORNING SONG

On the axis of my sleep
The world wheeled. Then dead noon
Could flame Rome and Asia:
My dark was deeper dawn.

If the alarm in night's wake
Curved westward, my caught eye
Looked up to kill the clock,
To quiet the crying day.

Those leaping omens, birds,
I silenced in their trees,
And held the million wheels
Locked in the dumb cities.

It was the only hour.
The still concentric spheres,
White magic, cool crystal,
Sang with the morning stars.

The damned themselves I saved.
The nothing of my dream
Sluiced neatly, bright as hell,
The shadiest cess of time.

Charmed, still that minute moved:
The stumbling sun came in
And broke both sky and pit.
The glass looked, bare as stone.

There is not one who sees.
My notebook, calendar,
My idiot suits and ties,
Burned in the empty air.

Then ships' and wings' shadows
On their great circles hung
Still while the tired sirens
Turned, ticking the same song.

Schooled, yawning like a dog,
My demon rose in wrath,
Slouched growling through the door
And stretched himself to death.

STRIKING A BALANCE

My desk heavy with ciphers
   I hear the house sleeping.
      In the next room

My children's monkeys and bears
   Sprawling at startled angles
      Sleep with eyes open;

They look through the walls
   And watch me learning to count.
      For, though the midnight

Is huge at the screen, flooding
   The room with vague rhetoric, still,
      According to schedule

The moon steps over the tree, and bows
   Gracefully through clouds, moving
      The tides of money.

I float like a juggler, spinning,
   Bouncing invisible dollars,
      Drawing checks on the dark,

Balancing the high cumulus
   Of monthly bills on the dull point
      Of a dwindling deposit,

Balancing the whole heaven of meaning
   Against my fraction that approaches
      Tomorrow's zero.

The moon has set and the Pleiades;
   How does a man move with the light
      And stay still at the center?

A hundred books, each dead
   With the wit of a master,
      Lean from their shelves,

Whispering to me in unison
   Their equidistant answers.
      The walls come closer;

The world is so contracted,
   A gnat would stifle in it;
      Now the stars are down,

The gentlest dewdrop, wrapped
   In the pink and green of sunrise,
      Is convulsed by the need

To kick in all directions
   Like an undisciplined grain
      Of dingy mustard.

To purge this taste from my pores
   I make for the shower:
      It is time to shave off

The grisly whiskers of darkness,
   To unwind the night watch,
      To break fast;

Dawn fingers the house,
   Searching the curtains,
      Changing the chairs.

Suddenly the children's voices
   Wake up like birds; the cat
      Uncoils herself;

My wife's yawn spreads slowly to
   A smile; it is time to scrub,
      To eat oatmeal;

To consider how to repair
   The rust in the fender, and relish
      Tomorrow's birthday.

Rejoicing like a bridegroom, the sun,
   Apollo, that prosperous banker,
      Physician and priest,

Is back in business, calm as a statue,
   Lending his world of gold on terms
      That are clear as daylight.

THE CATCH

That time when I went fishing
I bent under sea,
Then climbed the tide, the tepid river,
The icy steps of streams.

For bait I cast my skin
To catch the biting secret,
The trout whose light rainbow
Leaps the rock, the flood.

Skimming brook and pool,
The smallest of his scales
Would move a wicked mirror,
Now catching fire, now cooling

That world-eater, Leviathan,
Down to a flickering minnow,
Now glassing the naked soul
Flung from the blood's cataract.

So flashed the quarry I fished:
The buried quick of bread
Cast drowning on the water,
Always almost to touch,

But there in the green refraction
Lithe fish, gold shadows, sliding
Through loops like zeroes, twinkled
To nothing under my fingers,

Until with a sudden pull
Of gravity, strong as man's ghost
Out of the strangling dark
Stands forth in noon's being,

Sculptured, of marble or air,
My arm was right, my hand held:
It was the living catch, a fish
With money in his mouth,

Ready with water music,
While laughing I held him,
To sound and turn to a new light
The dark of the stone floor,

When salting prophecy woke
Under my nostrils, between my eyes;
Blood trickled my palate,
A hook sprang in my throat,

Its string stretched to a hand
Bent at the world's end,
The barb in my bone,
The iron root branching

Quick through the mouth's roof,
Time-stemmed, a breathing vine,
With light tendrils to thread
The labyrinth of my brain.

AT THE SHADOW'S HEART

Where you are still
It is as if a world
Were moving, hidden still

The secret trembling of air
The quickening of the silent stone

There stirs, hidden, the tree
That April hangs in strange air
That still streams upward from the rock

The presence of the breathing ghost
The grace that troubles the water

The winds in stillness surprise the rock pools
Stirring the fern's feather, the fiber of moss
To wake the light in deep shadows

The unseen quickening of danger
Time's death that quickens time

The heart grows still
Moving through rooms of darkness
Through the shade's labyrinth, the stone's heart

Threaded with roots of light
Slow, quickening the dark center

Beyond the mineral proof of mirrors
The mind's quicksilver, a tongue
Sings in the darkest fire

The quickening of the eye's fear
The knowledge that suffers face to face

Where you are still
Day's breath, earth's diamond, fire
Beyond the river's dark refraction

The quick, the still impossible
The pure transparence at the shadow's heart